ISLE ROYAL

LAKE SUPERIOR   DOMINION OF CANADA

SAULT DE STE

ONTONAGON

ONTONAGON

MARQUETTE

SCHOOLCRAFT

MACKINAC

ST. IGNACE

W I S C O N S I N

GREEN BAY

CHEBOYGAN

OTSEGO

MONT

L A K E   H U R O N

L A K E   M I C H I G A N

MANISTEE

MIDLAND

ARENA

SAGINAW BAY

SHEBOYGAN

LUDINGTON
PENTWATER

MECOSTA   ISABELLA

MILWAUKEE

MUSKEGON
GRAND HAVEN

RACINE

SAUGATUCK

INGHAM

LAKE
ST CLAIR

ILLINOIS

ST HAVEN

CANADA

BENTON HARBOR
ST JOSEPH

DETROIT

CHICAGO

MONROE   LAKE

NEW BUFFALO

I N D I A N A   O H I O   TOLEDO   ERIE

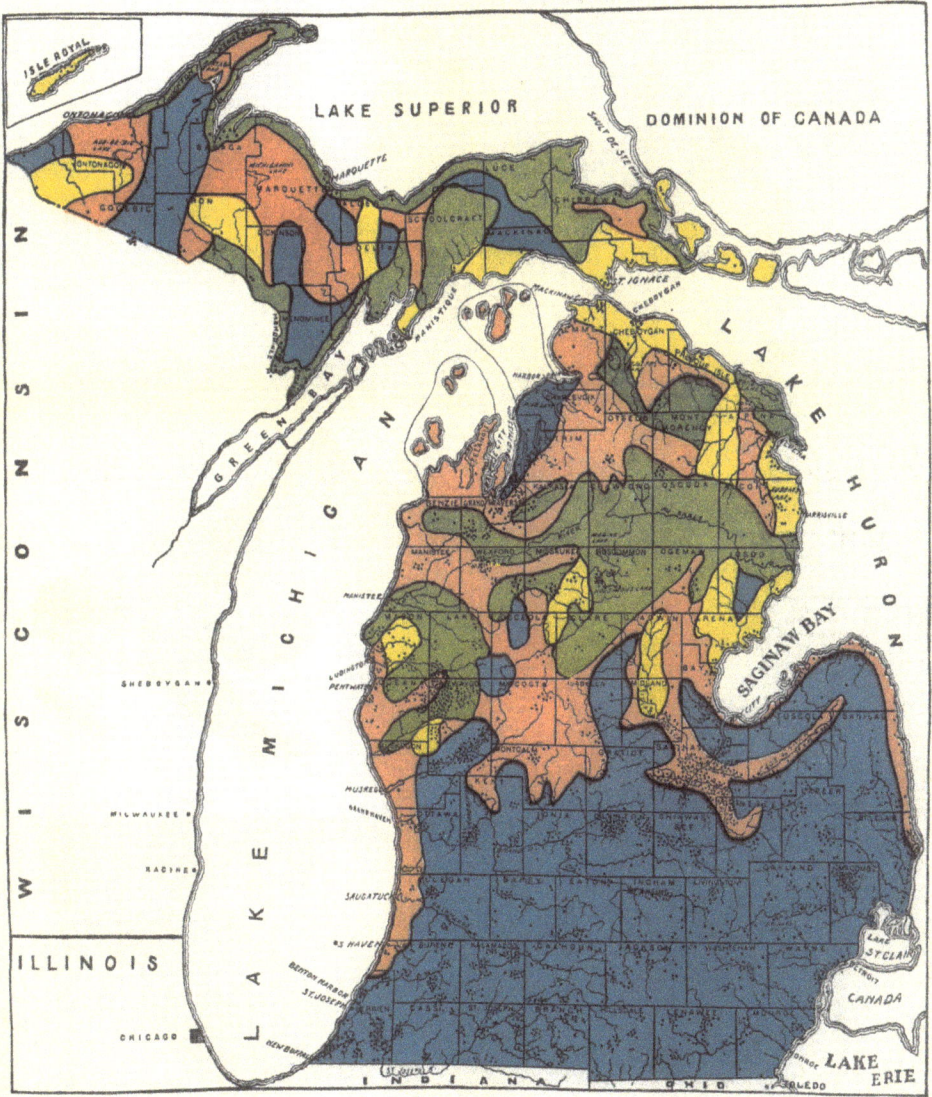

| | DECIDUOUS FOREST | | CONIFEROUS FOREST | | DECIDUOUS AND CONIFEROUS MIXED, DECIDUOUS PREDOMINATING | | CONIFEROUS AND DECIDUOUS MIXED, CONIFEROUS PREDOMINATING |

DISTRIBUTION OF INDIAN POPULATION OF MICHIGAN WITH REFERENCE TO THE NATURAL FORESTS, GREAT LAKES, AND STREAMS BEFORE AND DURING THE FIRST WHITE OCCUPANCY

POPULATION DISTRIBUTION AND THE COMPARATIVE FREQUENCY OF SITES ARE REPRESENTED BY DOTS

PRIMITIVE METHOD OF TAPPING MAPLE TREES
Scarification of tree; flat spile; and birch bark trough.

OCCASIONAL CONTRIBUTIONS FROM THE MUSEUM OF
ANTHROPOLOGY OF THE UNIVERSITY OF MICHIGAN
No. 2

DISTRIBUTION OF
THE ABORIGINAL POPULATION
OF MICHIGAN

BY

W. B. HINSDALE

ANN ARBOR, MICHIGAN
UNIVERSITY OF MICHIGAN PRESS
June 10, 1932

ISBN (print): 978-1-949098-61-7
ISBN (ebook): 978-1-951538-61-3

Browse all of our books at
sites.lsa.umich.edu/archaeology-books.

Order our books from the University of Michigan
Press at www.press.umich.edu.

For permissions, questions, or manuscript queries,
contact Museum publications by email at umma-
pubs@umich.edu or visit the Museum website at
lsa.umich.edu/ummaa.

ADVERTISEMENT

The publications of the Museum of Anthropology, University of Michigan, are made through the medium of a single series — the Occasional Contributions. The individual papers constituting this series are issued at irregular intervals as opportunity permits.

The Occasional Contributions are numbered serially, in the chronological order of their separate publication. When a sufficient number of pages have been printed to make a volume, a title page, index, and table of contents will be supplied to libraries and individuals on the mailing list for the series.

The subject matter of the individual contributions prepared by staff members and friends of the Museum includes descriptions of museum collections and field work, results of research, and discussions of field and museum techniques.

Carl E. Guthe
Director
Museum of Anthropology
University of Michigan

TABLE OF CONTENTS

DISTRIBUTION OF THE ABORIGINAL POPULATION OF MICHIGAN

ACKNOWLEDGMENTS

GRATEFUL acknowledgment is made to Mr. Lloyd R. Gates, Instructor in the Department of Hygiene and Public Health, of the University of Michigan, and to Miss Nellie Bosma, formerly of the Department of Zoology, University of Michigan, now at Beaver College, Jenkintown, Pennsylvania, for technical estimates upon food values; to Prof. Jethro O. Veach, Research Associate, Soils, Michigan State College, to Mr. Raphael Zon of the U. S. Department of Agriculture, whose maps entitled "Reconstruction of Original Forest Cover Based on Soil Maps" and the "Atlas of American Agriculture" respectively, have, with the map "Original Forests of Michigan" compiled from Land Office field notes, served as bases for my forest map entitled "Distribution of Indian Population of Michigan with reference to the natural forests, Great Lakes, and streams before and during the first white occupancy."

Special mention should be made of the kindness of Mr. Verne H. Church, Agricultural Statistician for Michigan, of the State Department of Agriculture, Lansing, Michigan, for permission to use his map entitled "Corn in Michigan 1919" appearing in *Michigan Agriculture — Statistical Analysis,* June 1, 1922, which indicates the distribution of corn culture in Michigan. The Department of Botany of the University of Michigan, the University Herbarium, the Division of Mammals, the Division of Birds, and the Division of Fishes of the Museum of Zoology, and the Division of Ethnology of the Museum of Anthropology have at various times responded to solicitations for information.

The colored map was drawn by Mr. Charles C. Mony, of the Department of Forestry of the University of Michigan. The frontispiece is from a drawing by Mr. Carleton W. Angell, Artist, University Museums, University of Michigan.

GENERAL STATEMENT

The Division of the Great Lakes of the Museum of Anthropology, as a part of its archaeological and ethnological survey of Michigan, has prepared an atlas recently published under the direction of the Executive Board of the Graduate School of the University of Michigan. *The Archaeological Atlas of Michigan* includes a series of maps which present, so far as it can be done graphically, the results of the surveys. One of the outstanding features of the maps of the different parts of the state, when they are assembled and arranged so as to present upon one large sheet the general situation, is the difference in the density of the Indian population, one section being compared with another. All kinds of sites sketched on the maps being taken together, villages, burying grounds, mounds, embankments, and other earth-works, in those districts where they occur the most thickly, the inference is that there the people were the most numerous.

Objection may be raised upon the ground that some sites should be given more significance than others as evidence of numbers. A village or burying ground is perhaps the most positive proof that people lived in a certain locality; whereas mounds or embankments might have been some distance from places of abode. Mounds almost invariably contain skeletons, perhaps remains of bodies that have been transported, but it is not likely that very great distances separated either mounds or inclosures from the camps of their builders.

It will be noted, from observing the situations charted upon the maps of the *Atlas*, that the state can be divided readily into population districts. The problem is to determine the causes for the inequality of distribution.

Out of the total of 2,152 sites of all kinds, definitely located, 1,026, or nearly 50 per cent, occur in 15 counties, the names and the numbers of sites of which follow: Newaygo, 159; Saginaw, 158; Berrien, 74; Grand Traverse, 69; Clinton, 65; Kalamazoo, 61; Kent, 59; Van Buren, 58; Genesee, 57; Oceana, 50; Macomb, 47; St. Joseph, 45; Mason, 42; Menominee, 41; St. Clair, 41.

The 15 counties in the following list, with a total of 400 sites identified, were the abode of about 22 per cent of the Indians: Calhoun, 38; Lenawee, 37; Branch, 36; Allegan, 36; Lapeer, 36; Shiawassee, 34; Tuscola, 33; Jackson, 30; Hillsdale, 30; Sanilac, 30; Cass, 29; Oakland, 28; Ionia, 28; Huron, 28; Wexford, 27. The 30 countries of this and the preceding group of the state's total of 83 counties sustained over 70 per cent of the natives.

The 15 counties of the following group, being the third group of "fifteens" out of the state's 83 counties, contained 15 per cent of the entire population: Antrim, 27; Montcalm, 27; Lake, 26; Alcona, 24; Livingston, 24; Roscommon, 23; Barry, 22; Missaukee, 22; Manistee, 22; Isabella, 21; Bay, 21; Wayne, 21; Washtenaw, 20; Midland, 19; Alpena, 19.

The 45 counties remaining, comprising about 46 per cent of the entire surface of the state, supported but 15 per cent of the population. If the map of population distribution is compared with the map of forest distribution of the state, it will be observed that the Indian had a decided preference for the deciduous forests. There are two or three seeming exceptions to this statement: for example, Newaygo County, which has the highest count of aboriginal sites of all the counties, was half covered with coniferous trees; and Lake, Roscommon, Missaukee, Manistee, and Wexford counties, which are also comprised within the groups of denser population, were districts where coniferous groves occupied a considerable part of the land surface. Reference to these conditions is made in the section on "Special Situations." There were occasional patches of conifers among the hardwoods, and the latter were sometimes interspersed with pines, hemlocks, spruce, and cedars. The inference must not be made that, because hardwoods were prevalent where Indians seem to have been the most numerous, the nature of the wood itself accounts for the larger population.

Streams and bodies of water, because they were usually well stocked with living things, were inviting to the natives. There were few water-living or water-frequenting animals that were not eaten. An Indian may have been a little fastidious about lizards and tadpoles, but when driven by hunger, as he found himself a considerable part of the time, little that he could masticate and swallow escaped his mouth. He may have been somewhat like Mother Goose's stork:

> When food began to fail,
> He would dine upon a snail.

Even a few larvae might postpone starvation. Beside fish, amphibians, and reptiles, there were thousands of waterfowl and some aquatic edible plants that materially affected population numbers. Some of the streams and lakes were almost gorged with fish, others did not have enough to attract attention. The Au Sable country, for instance, at first sight would appear to have been an ideal home for men of the canoe and the woods. Ichthyologists state that, before game fish were introduced into that stream, the kinds that were native to it, like the greyling, in the central and lower parts, were insufficient to afford much food. The stream may have been as beautiful scenically as it is to the present day tourist, but no one can maintain a home depending entirely upon scenery and sparkling water for subsistence. For over a hundred miles one could have traveled the valley of the Au Sable through the counties of Iosco, Oscoda, and Crawford, and probably not seen an Indian. These counties, comprising nearly 1,800 square miles, lie in what was the largest pine forest of the state. According to the maps showing distribution of habitations, but nine sites have been located in the entire region. The coniferous woods, pebbly-bottomed clear water, and the rapid streams were not frequented by many game animals, large fish, or water birds, nor did they produce wild rice.

It should be noted that the northernmost county that falls within the group of the most populous fifteen is Menominee. The explanation for this is that it lies in the wild rice belt. The wild rice harvest of one year determined the welfare of the people for the year ensuing.

One of the most populous sections of the state was in the southwest corner, in the part of the valley of the St. Joseph River which lies for the most part in Berrien County. It may be said that many of the villages and camps of that region were inside the historic period, and that the Indians assembled there on account of the numerous missions and posts, but it was not the custom for missionaries and traders to establish themselves where the population was sparse and to wait for the natives to come. If the Indians had not been numerous there in the first place, the chapels, schools, store houses, and forts would never have been built. One must find in the situation some natural reason for the St. Joseph drainage basin to have been so well adapted to a comparatively fixed and numerous population. Further reference is made to the St. Joseph Valley in the paragraphs upon "Special Situations."

The remarks of Dr. Lee R. Dice are pertinent in this connection, bearing in mind that man in the cultural status of the American Indian must be classified among the native mammals:

> . . . it has been shown that plants limit the distribution of mammals in many ways, also that plants are lim-

ited in distribution by some of the same factors which limit the distribution of mammals. Although mammals are in general very adaptable, and although many forms range over several vegetation types, there is a considerable amount of correlation between mammalian distribution and types of vegetation.[1]

POPULATION AND FOOD

The surface geology is one of the determining factors in a population; it is perhaps more so with primitive people than with those whose advanced cultures have overcome the lack of native products by means of transportation and commerce:

> The Lower Peninsula is covered with a deep drift of alternating sands, clays, and gravels, and the flora of any section depends chiefly on which of these happens to lie uppermost.[2]

Upon the quality and quantity of the vegetable growth of a territory depends the number of individuals it can support. The pine country proper, embracing 15,000 square miles, or nearly 418 townships, was composed largely of sand hills and plains. Where it was not covered with dense pine forest, there was a scarcity of vegetation. The area was limited roughly upon the north by a line from Thunder Bay, Alpena County, to Grand Traverse Bay, and upon the south by about the forty-third parallel. Occurring like oases in a desert, there were also argillaceous tracts wooded with beech and maple, swamps with tamaracks and other characteristic lowland timber, and forests of spruce and hemlock. There were occasional oak ridges. Jack pines were typical of the "barrens." Down the western part of the state, nearly to the Indiana line, due probably to a moister climate or

[1] Lee R. Dice, "The Relation of Mammalian Distribution to Vegetation Types," *Sci. Mon.* (Oct. 1931), 33:314.
[2] W. J. Beal, "Michigan Flora," Reprint from *Fifth Rept. Mich. Acad. Sci.* 1904, p. 13.

favorable soil, hemlock and spruce were well interspersed with hardwoods.[3]

North of the "pine belt" just mentioned, to the Straits of Mackinac, conifers were mixed with the deciduous, each kind usually occurring in large groves as the character of the soil varied. There were also extensive forests of both kinds of trees, covering in alternating, irregular tracts the Upper Peninsula.

It has been necessary to dwell tediously, and with some repetition upon the tree distribution of the state because the kinds of trees have a direct influence upon life, both human and animal. The Indians procured very little, if any, kind of food from conifers, although mention might be made that pine, spruce, hemlock, and cedar boughs made good bedding for the lodges; the roots, or *watap*, were used for strands and cords in joining barks together into canoes and hollow ware, the seams of which were rendered water-tight with the resins and gums. Animals whose flesh made human food could not subsist upon resinoid kinds of trees; whereas fruits, nuts, berries, sugars, building barks, and browse for some of the animals came from the other types of vegetable growth. The gloomy recesses of the pine woods, monotonous and scant in nutritional plants, were not often frequented by animal and bird life in appreciable numbers. That part of the state is so non-productive that, since it has been denuded of the pine, it has not afforded congenial conditions for people who subsist upon what they can force the soil to produce. (See map entitled "Corn in Michigan.")

A naturalist, who traversed in the interest of his science the pine woods of the state, narrates that occasionally a gopher or a lean red squirrel made an appearance. Under the root of a tree, once in a few miles, some fox that was sneaking upon a partridge or two had his burrow. In a day's

[3] W. J. Beal and C. F. Wheeler, "Michigan Flora," *Thirtieth Ann. Rept., Sec. State Board of Agriculture* (Lansing, Mich.), 1892, p. 486.

search, one would possibly strike the spoor of a deer or notice, upon the bark of a tree, where a bear had "measured" himself. Where the situation was favorable in the course of a stream, a few beavers might have made a meadow, but four-footed animals were exceedingly scarce.[4]

Where maple, beech, and oak predominated, the soil was more fertile and consequently afforded a richer growth of forage for animal life. Man, who consumes both vegetable foods and flesh, competed with the ruminants, rodents, and other plant-, fruit-, and seed-eaters, and kept their numbers somewhat in check, coöperating unconsciously in doing so with the sneaking carnivors who always trail the vegetarians.

The man-land ratio, for people in the hunting-agricultural stage of culture, as were the Michigan Indians, depends upon the productivity or fertility of the soil in regard to plant and animal products available for and convertible into human food. Such products are game, fish, wild edible vegetable products, and whatever was raised by woman's tillage with flint hoe and sharpened stick. Since the soil varied greatly in different parts, the population could not have have been uniform, as the surveys have demonstrated.

Sir Arthur Keith makes the following statement:

> A tribe numbering fifty souls, if it depends for a livelihood on the natural produce of soil and river, needs a fertile territory measuring 100 square miles for its subsistence. If it cultivates only a one-hundredth part of its territory in a crude manner it can easily quadruple its numbers, whereas the surrounding hunting tribes living up to the limits of available food remain stationary.[5]

One cannot safely make this a rule for particular estimates because fertility of territory varies in degree.

[4] L. H. Dewey, "Animal Life in the Pine Woods," *Twenty-Seventh Ann. Rept. of the Sec. of the State Board of Agriculture of the State of Michigan*, July 1, 1887 to June 30, 1888, pp. 187-188.
[5] Sir Arthur Keith, "The Greatest Test For Mankind," *The New York Times Magazine*, Sunday, February 8, 1931.

While it is instructive to study numbers in regard to expanse of territory from which sustenance is gathered, it is equally interesting to make estimates of the quantity and quality of the food required. Beside the other hazards to which they were constantly exposed, without doubt the length of the Indian's life was shortened because of the excessive richness of his diet in proteins during long periods of the year, and also by the mineral and vitamin deficiency. His diet during certain periods of the year and when away from his beaten paths, depended largely upon chance.

It seems to be agreed by physiologists that a man at moderately hard work requires somewhat more than 3,000 calories for each day. Food quantity may fluctuate above and below this average, but there is a minimum below which a man cannot survive the effects of malnutrition and be adequate to care for himself. It can be safely assumed that the calorie necessity of men of different races is very much the same, weight for weight. If then 3,000 calories are allowed for each full-grown Indian man, and if it be assumed, for calculation, that he consumed only the one kind of food, according to the food values, he would require daily 6.7 pounds of fish; twice as many pounds of clams; 2.6 pounds of lean beef, buffalo, deer meat, or other game or wild fowls. He might eat 1.9 pounds of maple sugar, the equivalent of which in fat is about 13 ounces; 1.8 pounds of corn meal, dried legumes, shelled nuts, or seeds; 11 pounds of fresh berries, fruits, roots, or greens, one third less than that amount if dried. Of course, the nutritional value of berries, the same as with other classes of foods, varies somewhat. Huckleberries and blueberries are among the "richest," and strawberries, on account of their greater water content, among the lowest. The nutritional value of wild rice, so important a food in many sections, and which materially influenced population, is .879 as compared with corn.

Although the Michigan Indians knew nothing about potatoes, it is interesting to note, in this connection, that when the Irish, by force of famine and other circumstances, subsisted almost entirely upon them (1846):

> . . . the daily average consumption of an able-bodied labourer in Ireland was estimated at nine-and-a-half pounds of potatoes for men, and seven-and-a-half for women.[6]

At this rate a bushel of potatoes would last a man about a week.

According to the United States Census for 1830, which is taken because it is assumed that the whites, being at that time overwhelmingly rural, would have approximately about the same percentage of children, women, and men, as the Indian population, Sir Arthur Keith's primitive "tribe" of 50 individuals would consist of about 22 children, 14 women, and 14 men.   If the average adult, arguing from the army rations of the civilized world, requires a thousand pounds of dry foodstuff per year,[7] it would be necessary for the tribe to collect annually enough material to yield, when "dry," 36,200 pounds, or over 18 tons, in order to maintain physical vigor.   In making this computation, a woman's consumption is reckoned at 80 per cent and an average child's (fourteen or under) as 50 per cent of that of an adult man.

It must be considered that the estimate above is for dry foodstuffs well prepared for converting into edible form. The unprepared amount collected was at least more than as much again: animals with their skins, horns, bones, hoofs, and offal; fish with heads, fins, scales, and other refuse; and corn, nuts, and many other products with husks, shells, and cobs.   This is an average of about four pounds per day for each man, woman, and child, according to proportions given above.[8]

---

[6] Henry Thomas Buckle, *History of Civilization in England* (New York, 1894), 1:48, (footnote).

[7] Edward M. East, *Mankind at the Crossroads* (Scribner's, New York, 1923), p. 67.

[8] Julius Friedenwald and John Ruhräh, *Diet in Health and Disease,* (W. B. Saunders & Co., Philadelphia, 1925), p. 779 (table).

Not more than half the persons engaged in collecting materials for subsistence, the other half having been composed of small children, the aged, and the incompetent. The collectors, were they hunters, fishermen, or plant-, nut-, root-, or grain-gatherers, had to average each a daily contribution of eight pounds to the community's rations, or about a ton and a half annually. Besides this, there must be added to the labors of the "bearers of burdens," materials for lodges, clothing, bedding, fire, and defenses, and a considerable amount of water. A range of 100 square miles for supplies for 50 persons was altogether inadequate in more than half the territory of Michigan, as is shown elsewhere. Under conditions in which what was consumed was equal to what was possessed, there could be no residue or "capital," the accumulation of which is one of the first steps above the cultural grade in which the Indians lived. It has been said:

> Wherever savages have been visited in their native simplicity, they seem to have found out just how to garner the products of plants in the best manner.[9]

The narrative of David Thompson written about 1798, is very informing as to the population of the south side of Lake Superior. He was an excellent traveler and an exceedingly accurate and methodical surveyor. A part of his life work was performed as Astronomer to the International Boundary Commission. Under the Treaty of Ghent, he surveyed the boundary line between British North America and the United States from where the forty-fifth parallel of latitude strikes the St. Lawrence River to the northwest angle of the Lake-of-the-Woods:

> The survey we had finished was of the south side, from the west, to the east end; following the shores, the distance is 671 miles, but the direct line is only 383 miles. We had met with 110 families, and allowing twenty families not seen, will give 130 families. Mr. Cadotte,

[9] Otis T. Mason, *The Origins of Invention: A Study of Industry Among Primitive Peoples*, (Charles Scribner's Sons, New York, 1895), p. 190.

who was for many years a Trader in these parts, thought 125 families to be nearer the number. Allowing these Natives to have possession of hunting ground only to the distance of 70 miles from the Lake, the extent will be 26,810 square miles, and this divided by 130 will give to each family an extent of 206 square miles of hunting ground; yet with this wide area, the annual average hunt of each family of all kinds of furrs, from the Bear down to the Musk Rat, will not exceed sixty to seventy skins in trade; allowing a Bear skin to be the value of two beavers; and eight to ten musk Rats to be the value of one beaver. Deer are so scarce that all they kill does not furnish leather for their wants, and when the mild seasons come they all descend to Lake Superior to live by fishing.[10]

His "usual rule" was to allow seven persons to a family. The total population of a strip of land seventy miles wide along the entire south side of Lake Superior would have been, according to Thompson's calculations, 875 individuals, not more than 650 of whom lived in what is now Michigan. Moreover, the seventy-mile strip would include almost all of the Northern Peninsula and, granting the correctness of his estimate, the Indian population of that section of the state, in 1800, was about 700.

IMPORTANT SOURCES OF FOOD

ANIMAL

Quadrupeds—The Indians have always been regarded as a race of hunters and it is true that they subsisted very largely upon what is usually called "game." Probably every kind of quadruped that ever lived in the state was eaten, provided it happened to be caught. There are some animals that are usually regarded as "game" which signifies those worthy of the sportsman's attention. Among the "big" game the American bison or buffalo stands out prominently when

[10] *David Thompson's Narrative of His Explorations in Western America, 1784-1812,* Ed. by J. B. Tyrrell (Toronto, The Champlain Society, 1916), pp. 297-298.

the Indians of the western United States are considered. The buffalo was a grassland animal and avoided thick timberland. There are authentic records of the buffalo having come into the forest openings of the southern counties, but it was nowhere sufficiently abundant to influence materially the permanent locations of Indian hunting groups. The elk was distributed over the Lower Peninsula but seems to have avoided the pine lands. It contributed of its flesh, horns, and bones to the Indian's larder and tool chest.

In the Upper Peninsula and in the southeastern quarter of the Lower Peninsula, moose abounded, but they probably were not numerous enough except north of the Straits of Mackinac for the Indians to depend upon moose flesh for more than an occasional fortuitous luxury.[11] Father Joseph Jouvency, S. J., says of the moose:

> The savages eat its flesh, are clothed with its skin, and are cured by the hoof of its left hind leg.[12]

The common deer, one might say, was a perennial "stand-by" as an important food supply through the deciduous forests of the Lower Peninsula. While this animal is common north of the Straits of Mackinac at the present time, formerly it was very scarce.[13]

The beaver was among the creatures that made the streams attractive to the natives. It yielded a generous (if nature was ever generous) quantity of food and the best furs for clothing that the world afforded. Where bears could find enough to eat, they were common. They had about the same ranges and fed upon about the same food as the Indian, and, in turn, contributed their carcasses to his commissary and their skins for bedcovers. Bear's fat was a

[11] Norman A. Wood, from his personal record map showing "Distribution of Moose in Michigan," compiled from earliest accounts to the present time.

[12] *The Indians of North America*, sel. and ed. by Edna Kenton (Harcourt, Brace, and Co., New York, 1927), 1:4.

[13] See David Thompson, *op. cit.*, p. 298.

most delicious and appetizing delicacy to the Indian's taste.

All the small animals, when they could be captured, helped to appease hunger. Among them may be mentioned the snowshoe and cottontail rabbits, the porcupine, muskrat, raccoon, badger, and otter. The following estimates indicate the length of time animals of average weight, after being prepared for cooking, would last a village of 50 persons estimated upon figures given before: moose, 5 days; elk, 4 days; bear, 2 days. Two common deer or 40 snowshoe rabbits would be consumed daily.

It might not have occurred very often that subsistence was confined for very long periods to flesh alone, but the estimates given upon the supposition that such circumstances did arise, may be instructive. I have already mentioned that a diet too rich in nitrogenous elements shortens life. In this connection, the statement of Dr. George Grant MacCurdy as to the food supply of man prior to the Neolithic Period may be pertinent:

> In Switzerland during the last interglacial epoch it [food] was ninety per cent cave bear; in Moravia during the last glacial epoch it was ninety per cent mammoth; in Denmark during the Mesolithic Period it was ninety per cent shell fish.[14]

To indicate the game resources of parts of the state available to the native Indians, the statistics given below are submitted. They are based upon authenticated records compiled in 1878, a time when many animals, birds, and fish had not been materially depleted in numbers. The figures impress one with the rather rich "meat" supply that was always available, in sections where animals abounded, to the dusky hunters who never pursued the animals for sport or took more than they could consume. No game laws, except Indian "common law," or wardens were necessary in those "barbarous" times.

[14] George Grant MacCurdy, *Prehistoric Man* (American Library Association, Chicago, 1928), p. 30.

In 1877 the grand total of venison shipments in Michigan, during the two short months in which the weather permitted the transportation of deer, was 1,070,000 pounds of which 850,000 were shipped outside the state. This slaughter totals for a 60-day season 10,700 carcasses. In one season, 6,000 pounds, or 3 tons of game birds, mostly partridges, were shipped from one city of 10,000 inhabitants alone. From the nesting places of pigeons:

> . . . in Newaygo, Oceana, and Grand Traverse counties, in 1875, were shipped to outside markets 1,000 tons, or 2,000,000 pounds of young 'squabs;' while not less than 200,000 dozen, or 2,400,000 birds were entrapped and shipped to all parts of the United States and England.[15]

This kind of inhuman slaughter went on every season for many years and shows most clearly the animal food resources the Indians had, in certain sections, to draw upon.

A party of two gentlemen and two ladies who encamped upon a stream for about a fortnight caught 3,000 greylings, 2,000 of which were taken to Chicago, the other 1,000 not being in sufficiently good state of preservation to be transported. Another party from Chicago caught, during an expedition of 4 weeks, 5,000 greylings.[16] The greyling is today almost an extinct fish in Michigan waters.

Fish—With over 1,100 miles of great lake frontage, containing more than 4,187 lakes covering 500 square miles and traversed by many rivers by means of which, with portages of a few miles, the state could be crossed from east to west in the Lower, and from north to south in the Upper Peninsula, there is marked contrast with all other sections of the country. Few parts of the world were so well supplied with unlimited numbers of fresh-water fish, some

---

[15] H. B. Roney, "The Importance of More Effective Legislation for the Protection of Game and Fish," *Mich. Sportsmen's Assoc. for the Protection of Fish, Game, and Birds,* 1878.

[16] *Ibid.*

kinds of enormous size. Fish had perhaps more influence in determining the distribution of the Indians than game or other forest or open land food resources, which is the same as saying the lands contiguous to the waters were usually preferred situations for abodes.

The largest fish known to Michigan waters is the sturgeon which has an average weight of 60 pounds and a maximum of about 150 pounds. Sturgeon abounded in the bays of the Great Lakes in immense numbers and ascended the rivers fifty or sixty miles, or as far as their bulky bodies permitted. At the Sault Ste. Marie, and in other similar channels, white fish were so plentiful in season that the number caught was limited only by the facilities, which were very crude and awkward before white man's tackle came into the Indian's hands.

Pike, pickerel, dogfish, lake trout, muskellunge, bass, bullheads, and gars were common in the large lakes and rivers. Suckers and sheepheads mingled more or less with the rest of the finny tribe in the streams. In the inland lakes all kinds of fish known to the northern sportsman were very much more numerous than at present. Seasonal variation of the waters and the search for breeding places caused the fish that were not land-locked to disappear in one place to appear in another. In the winter, ice made many of the waters sealed reservoirs not so easily broken open with the Indian's clumsy implements. When fish could not be secured, the fishermen became hunters and removed inland in search of game.

Periodical removal from the forest to the lake shore was a habit of the Chippewa especially of the Upper Peninsula. Such having been the circumstances, there were probably many villages or encampments that were unoccupied for parts of the year. The custom of having summer and winter residences dates well back into primitive times. To be able to remain in one home the year around was a mark of prosperity.

Among the animals living in the water all or most of the time, turtles, frogs, and clams must not be overlooked. Clams deserve special mention as the people made many a feast of them upon the banks of streams and shores of lakes to which fact the refuse piles of shells, in some places still attest.   To maintain the village of 14 men, 14 women, and 22 children entirely upon fish, there would be required, for adequate nourishment, 7 sturgeon of the average size of 60 pounds, or 150 black bass each weighing, coming from the water, 3 pounds, or 234 pounds of "dressed" fish daily, and, if the subsistence were to consist entirely of clams, twice that number of pounds would be required.

Birds—Attracted by the thousands of lakes and the numerous rivers of the state, myriads of migratory water birds, from ponderous swans to least sandpipers, were available in the spring and autumn to the Indians.   The almost endless flocks of passenger pigeons that frequented, in their season of migration and breeding, the hardwood belts, especially those containing beech and oak, must have furnished abundant food for the Indians while their season lasted.   The birds and their squabs were easily killed at night at their nesting places which, in some localities, covered hundreds of acres.   One pigeon roost in Emmet County included at least 100,000 acres.[17]

Wild turkeys and grouse were very numerous in the hardwood ranges and thickets and were non-migratory.   It must be constantly borne in mind that the Indians, depending upon bow and arrow, stone axes, flint knives, clumsy fish spears, and a few devices for trapping, had but a chance for the success that came with guns, steel axes and knives, fish hooks, nets, and steel traps.   The eggs of wild birds were easy to gather and no doubt filled many an empty stomach, but everything had its season, and stomachs went empty

[17] Walter Bradford Barrows, *Michigan Bird Life* (Michigan Agricultural College, 1912), p. 245.

longer as the game shifted, the birds ceased to lay eggs and flew away to their summer haunts, and the water froze.

During certain parts of the year the food supply was more than enough to sustain its dependents, but the pinch came during "the long and dreary Winter! The cold and cruel Winter" when:

> Hardly from his buried wigwam
> Could the hunter force a passage;
> With his mittens and his snow-shoes
> Vainly walked he through the forest,
> Sought for bird or beast and found none,
> Saw no track of deer or rabbit.

The time when the suffering was the greatest and the death toll probably the largest was before the spring "break" came, when there was no transient wandering migratory bird, the ice on lake and river was the thickest, the wild animals were the thinnest in both numbers and flesh, the caches of food were exhausted, and the smoked and dried meats and fish were gone. The stored supplies were seldom adequate for the stress and rigor of prolonged cold, and the Indian's improvidence seems never to have been corrected by repeated experiences. The winter restricted the population:

> . . . the hunter can fight no more against the nipping cold and blinding sleet. Stiff and stark, with haggard cheek and shrivelled lip, he lies among the snowdrifts; till, with tooth and claw, the famished wildcat strives in vain to pierce the frigid marble of his limbs.[18]

Schoolcraft comments that:

> . . . there are few animals which the Indians reject as food. . . . I have heard, however, that crows and vultures are not eaten, but when they are pushed to hunger, whatever can sustain life is taken.[19]

[18] Francis Parkman, *The Conspiracy of Pontiac and the Indian War after the Conquest of Canada* (Boston, Little, Brown & Co., 1910), 1:40.

[19] Henry R. Schoolcraft, *Personal Memoirs of a Residence of Thirty Years with the Indians* (Lippincott, Grambo, and Co., Philadelphia, 1851), p. 275.

When starvation confronted them, niceties about clan emblems and totems were also waived with apology or ceremony; which brings to mind King David's eating, under stress, the shew-bread sanctified only to the holy priests.

Herbaceous Plants—The discovery of cooking, in the evolution of man's diet, made long before the time of our Indians, led to an increase in the amount of starch entering the human stomach, and agriculture also tended to make men vegetarians and independent of animal food.[20]

The list of plants that yielded food for the Indians would be a long one, but it might be interesting to note that some plants native to Michigan that deserve more than a catalogued mention are thorn apples, pawpaws, mandrakes, plums, berries, crab apples, grapes, nuts, and cherries. These may be called plants of lost opportunity. If they had received the attention of men sufficiently advanced in pomology to develop them, as were developed the apples, plums, pears, grapes, and the other highly artificially specialized Old World types, they would probably have become as useful to mankind generally as any of the fruits. Dr. Asa Gray believes:

> . . . our ground-nut *(Apios tuberosa)* would have been the first developed esculent tuber, and would probably have held its place in the first rank along with potatoes and sweet potatoes of later acquisition.[21]

The following is a partial list of wild fruits, berries, nuts, and roots which together with corn, squashes, and maple sugar afforded the Michigan Indians 95 per cent of their non-animal food: serviceberries, pawpaws, the hickories, hazelnuts, chestnuts, beechnuts, strawberries, huckle-

[20] Harry Campbell, "The Evolution of Man's Diet," *The Lancet*, Sept. 17, 1904 (London), p. 851.
[21] W. J. Beal and C. F. Wheeler, *op. cit.*, p. 515.

berries, walnuts, May-apples, mulberries, the various wild
plums, gooseberries, raspberries, blackberries, cranberries,
grapes, dewberries, elderberries, crab apples, apios, hog pea-
nuts, sunflowers, hips and haws, wild cherries, acorns, seeds
of some of the grasses and other plants, sagittaria, many of
the fungi, and different succulent stems and tops of green
plants as pot-herbs for seasoning and flavors.

The preparations of foods from poisonous and acrid
bulbs, making them palatable by boiling and treatment with
alkalies, are complexes in cookery involving the knowledge
of their dangerous properties in the raw state and much skill
in making them tolerable. The wild crab was the only apple
known to the Indians before cultivated varieties were introduced by the whites. It is an excellent "keeper"; after being
buried or cached in the ground over winter it is considerably
toned down in astringency. Cakes were made from acorn
meal and even so pungent a tuber as wild turnip was rendered good to eat.[22] The following is a partial list of plants
cooked as greens: adder's-tongue, bellwort, ferns (many
species), lupine, trillium, poke root, Solomon's seal, cress,
and wild garlic. Sweet flag and wild onion were used as
flavors and "relishes." Many plants, some of them repug-
nant to smell like skunk cabbage and of acrid taste like Jack-
in-the-pulpit, were probably used as medicines. The Indians' pharmacopoeia included innumerable things swal-
lowed in mass and in mixtures that were imagined to have
healing virtues. Some plants were highly prized as dyes,
others for their fragrance. How much the Indians cherished
the wild flowers on account of their beauty seems not to have
received particular attention by those early writers who had
opportunity to observe, but it is known that for some reason
many plants owe their extended distribution to the influence
of the natives. It is also true that all living things were
regarded with deferential respect and in many instances

[22] Huron H. Smith "Ethnobotany of the Ojibwe Indians," *Bull Pub. Mus.
Milwaukee*, 4:402.

with actual veneration. The Indians could not endure ruth-
less destruction of any of the objects of nature, animate or
inanimate. They were the first and most scrupulous con-
servationists. They thought it improbable that Hell, as
described to them by the missionaries, was a place where
fire burned eternally because there would not only be a great
waste of timber but, they argued, the woods could not last
that long.[23] It must be realized that:

> . . . the relation of a people, especially of a primitive
> people, to their floral environment is obviously fundamen-
> tal to all their culture. This consideration is of the utmost
> importance for a clear understanding and a fair appraisal
> of economic conditions and of traits of material culture.[24]

Wild rice, the "precious gift of nature to the natives,"
had considerable influence in determining home sites. It was
common through the state in mud-bottomed lakes and slug-
gish streams and was very prevalent in the southern part of
Lake Superior, in Green Bay, St. Clair flats and river, Grand,
Huron, Kalamazoo, Raisin, Crooked, Cheboygan, St. Joseph,
Muskegon, Manistee, Thunder Bay rivers or parts of them,
and other waters of similar character.

The Indians wished to reserve the rice in their treaties.
It was one of the few grains that they planted. The Chippewa especially were acquaculturalists. The Menominee,
whose name signifies "wild rice people," depended upon the
extensive growth of the plant in Green Bay for a considerable part of their subsistence. In fact, as mentioned elsewhere, Menominee County would not have been among the
most thickly inhabited parts of the state had it not been
for the rice crops the people were able to gather. The dietary
of the Menominee was about as follows:

> In the spring they subsist on sugar and fish; in the sum-
> mer, on fish and game; in the fall, on wild rice and corn,

[23] See *The Indians of North America, op. cit.*, 1:17.
[24] Melvin R. Gilmore, "Importance of Ethnobotanical Investigation,"
Am. Anthrop., April-June, 1932, 34 (No. 2): 320.

and in the winter on fish and game. Those who are provident have some rice during the winter. The fish, consisting principally of sturgeon and salmon-trout, are in the greatest abundance in the bay.[25]

In seasons when the crop was poor, much suffering prevailed among the rice-gatherers. According to W. W. Warren, the rice fields were esteemed as the most valuable tribal property and were vigorously defended.[26] Quarrels over the privileges of harvesting the wild rice in Green Bay and contiguous waters often broke out into open warfare among the Michigan and Wisconsin tribes.[27]

The Indians east of the Rocky Mountains, living where there were a hundred continuous days of frost-free weather, when the fertility of soils permitted, carried on a considerable agriculture which was, no doubt, influenced by scarcity of game and other wild food products.

The crops of corn at many times were the sustaining part of the food of the Indians of Michigan. This was a forest country excepting a considerable area of swamp, a few small prairies, in all comprising about 80,000 acres in the counties of Berrien, Cass, St. Joseph, Branch, Kalamazoo, Calhoun, Barry, Eaton, and Newaygo, and some thinly timbered tracts called "oak openings."

The land had to be cleared before it could be planted. With the clumsy implements of the Indians, the process of making the soil arable was laborious and very slow. To make clearings with stone axes, celts, flint blades, and scrapers could, at best, result in only a very small tract being brought into cultivation annually. By girdling, or some other method, a few trees could be killed one year, and, by

[25] Walter James Hoffman, "The Menomini Indians," *Fourteenth Ann. Rept. Bur. Amer. Ethnol.* 1892-93, Part I (Wash. 1896), pp. 290-291.

[26] William W. Warren, "History of the Ojibway Nation," *Coll. of the Minn. Hist. Soc.*, 5:309-310.

[27] For an extended discussion see A. E. Jenks, "The Wild Rice Gatherers of the Upper Lakes," *Nineteenth Ann. Rept. Bur. Amer. Ethnol.*, 1897-1898, Pt. II, pp. 1019-1126.

CORN IN MICHIGAN

Crops of corn raised by farmers of the state represent very well the fertility of the soil. Where corn yields an indifferent crop the land is so nonproductive that it could never have furnished enough to sustain more than a small number of either animals or men if subsistence depended mainly upon vegetable growth.

burning the dry dead wood the next, ground could be made ready for the corn planting among the charred stubs, stumps, and trunks. An Indian clearing was little more than a spot in the woods where there was no leafy shade.

If one makes allowances for the differences in tools and the lack of traction animals, it is evident that to have cleared even a small part of the forests, an acre or two, must have required a degree of perseverance and energy upon the part of the Indians equal to that displayed by the whites who came to possess their lands.

Preparing the soil and planting the seeds were by no means all of the cultivation. The ceaseless contest against weeds had to be kept up in order that there might be any grain to harvest. The greater part of the state is not good corn land. Even under white cultivation a record kept for three consecutive years does not show an average yield of over 32.8 bushels per acre. Probably under the tillage of the Indian women, who were the planters of seeds and the exclusive manipulators of the soil, there was not raised more than 15 bushels per acre and the "patches" were, per family, very small. The population was more or less mobile. When a lake became "fished out," a corn tract sterile, or game scarce, there was but slight hindrance to removal of the village to a more congenial situation.

Population was sometimes indirectly influenced by local meteorological occurrences. At first thought it might seem that violent and destructive wind storms, if they had any influence would, in parts where they prevailed, deter rather than invite settlement. The Indians regarded the falling of timber and uprooting of trees as acts of spirits or supernatural powers, and their immediate impulse would be to leave or avoid the scene of a tornado. In time they might recover from the fright and be benefited after all. A good wind storm broke the monotony of sombre life. If, instead of the trees being killed with laborious effort, a violent cyclonic storm helped out the planter and laid the trees low, causing what is called a windfall, the next year the fallen wood was dry enough to be cleared away by fire and the ground became a cornfield. Such was nature's short cut, and the Indians profited thereby.

Between the years 1822 and 1856, before the white man's axe had deforested the lands, the deputy United States surveyors reported from the various parts of the state over 200 windfalls from a half-mile to several miles in extent. We may safely assign to devastating storms a facilitating influence in Indian agriculture. It was the "Thunderbird's" contribution to the welfare of the people.

Although tobacco was not a part of the food products of Indian agriculture, it formed an important function in social, medical, and religious ceremonies and customs. If there be some doubt that the plant was cultivated in Michigan, there is abundance of proof that the natives were addicted to smoking. In almost every part of the state pipes have been found upon old sites and haunts. These pipes are so various in design, workmanship, and material that they warrant the conclusion that they were lost or buried by groups quite distinct from each other. These is no stronger evidence that tribes or bands of different culture traits lived in the state than the models of the smoking pipes they have left, which vary from those of the typical Hopewell culture to the elbow clay pipes common in parts of Canada.

Of course tobacco was not the only fibre smoked. The barks and leaves of dogwoods, sumacs, willows, jimson weeds, and some woods, were used by some people for adulterating, or as substitutes for, tobacco. *Kinnikinnick*, an Algonquian word, was applied to the mixture. If tobacco was not a cultivated crop in this section of the country, it could have been easily obtained through the channels of primitive trade.

Trees and Shrubs—Any large tree from which the bark could be stripped in wide and long sheets was desirable as a source for "roofing" and "siding" for the lodges. A village had to be located with some reference to an available supply of "building" bark. The white birch was a precious tree. Its bark was a potential supply for a roof and for a canoe, and due to its pliability it was made into innumerable utensils as buckets, pails, cups, basins, and trays. A grove of birch stood in about the same relation to an Indian village as the sawmill and tin shop did to the pioneers. Cedar bark, elm, hemlock, and basswood made good shelters. The elms were common throughout the state, whereas the white birches, in large sizes, were scarce below the central parts.

The fibres called "bast," from the inside of the bark of some trees and found in excellent quality and quantity in basswood, were very important for making coarse bags, mats, for weaving, sewing, lacing, and for similar purposes. In almost any kind of handiwork in which strings, twines, and cordage were employed, bast was of the greatest use. The basswood should be included among the important trees. Black ash was desirable because it easily "worked up" into very thin strips that "run with the grain" for basketry and coarse matting. Willow sprouts, on account of their pliability, were woven into containers and wattles. White ash, the same as cedar wood, was excellent material for boat paddles and bows. The tough bark of moosewood, when fresh, made thongs as strong as leather.

The Indian had to exercise choice in the selection of firewood. For fires inside the lodges, woods, particularly hemlock, tamarack, the pines, spruce, balsams, box elder, cedars, and sassafras, that were liable to snap, were dangerous as the flying sparks might be the cause of burning down the dwelling.

Early travelers who have left accounts of their observations frequently refer to maple sugar as having been an important item in the Indian's food supply. After a few white man's utensils were obtained, the making of sugar, in season, was no doubt an important industry. The evidence that the Indians made maple sugar before that time is more inferential than positive, but the strong presumption is, they had fully developed the sugar-making complex and only lacked facilities for its further development.[28]

The process of evaporating sap in any container the Indians had must have been slow. None of their earthen pots were of sufficient size for boiling any amount. The suggestion that evaporation was accomplished by putting hot stones into large bark vats of sap does not appear at all practicable, even if possible, for the waste due to the viscosity of the syrup would have been great. One thing is certain: many of the writers who have discussed the making of maple sugar evidently never saw the process going on and knew little about "sugar weather." For example, one says the trees were "opened" when the crows began to caw in the spring, whereas sap only "runs" when the temperature of the day is above 32° and at night it is slightly below. Occasional warm rains and flurries of soft snow are typical of good sugar weather. The flow of sap is regulated by the weather conditions in the early spring and not by the cawing of crows, the day of the month, or any other signs. A "run" of sap will last from two or three days to a week and then be suspended by freezing or dry cold winds, to start up again when the weather "softens" with alternating day-and-night thaws and freezes. So soon as the buds of the maple trees are well started the season is over because the sap loses its sweet properties and can not be converted into syrup or sugar.

Sugar was shaped into cakes by the Indians or granulated by being stirred while in a hot and fluid state with a "sugar paddle." It was an excellent form in which to store energy and, when mixed with other foods, it added to their flavor and value. It was frequently crushed with parched corn and made a very appetizing and nutritious coarse meal

[28] H. W. Henshaw, "Indian Origin of Maple Sugar," *Am. Anthrop.* 3:341-351.

well adapted to transportation upon long journeys. Box
elder and birch trees also yielded a small amount of sweet
sap convertible into sugar.

Some of the tribes reverenced the maple, which really is
the dominating tree of the state, and performed formal ceremonies before tapping it. John Tanner says they called the
maple "our own tree." [29] One maple was of more account
in the Indian's economy than acres of white pine, spruce, or
hemlock.

An Ottawa chief, in commenting upon a treaty which
had been made in the Chippewa district, expressed himself
by saying that his people had no objections to the white
man's working the mines, cutting the timber, and making
farms, but they reserved the birch and cedar for canoes, the
rice, the sugar trees, and the privilege of hunting without
being disturbed by the whites.[30] S. W. Higgins, topographer
to the Geological Survey, reported to Douglass Houghton,
Michigan's first state geologist:

> No tree is held in higher estimation, by the Indians, than
> the sugar maple, and no source of complaint is more griev-
> ous, than a separation from it, by removal to places where
> it is not found.[31]

In a rough way, the population of the state can be checked
by noting the occurrences of maple trees.

Alexander Henry describes sugar making as he saw it
carried on among the Indians in 1763 just west of the
Sault. The sap was stored in vats each containing about
one hundred gallons. The women gathered in the sap, at-
tended to the boiling, and did the "sugaring off." The men
were none the less busy in securing wood for the fires and in
keeping up the food supply for the camp by hunting and
fishing. In the season, sugar was the principal food. The

[29] *Ibid.*, 3:349.
[30] Albert E. Jenks, *op. cit.*, p. 1096.
[31] *Documents Accompanying the Journal of the Senate, State of Michigan, at the Ann. Session,* 1840, 2:96.

Indians lived upon it, according to his story, for long periods of time.[32]

Some of the trees, such as yielded sugar and bore nuts, berries, and fruits, afforded an annual revenue and became more useful as they grew older, but those that were used for building and fuel or whose timber and bark were employed in some other economy of the people had but one "dividend to declare" and sacrificed their lives doing it.

SPECIAL SITUATIONS

Any territorial unit, whether township, county, or state, marked off by arbitrary, artificial, political lines is inconvenient for this kind of study. Natural situations make locations attractive as places of abode, and when they are grouped the boundaries do not turn at geometrical angles or run in straight lines; they are crooked, conforming to limitations imposed by the natural features of the country. Inside the boundaries of a few counties are some situations that deserve special mention.

The natives seldom lived in isolated families for very long. They had learned through long periods of experience that security and well-being depended upon close social and community relations, and naturally they assembled into villages. The factors that influenced the selection of a site were various. Probably no Indian, as founder of a village, ever reasoned out in detail why he established his followers in a certain spot, but he was guided none the less by favorable features of the immediate situation. In the first place, a supply of water was necessary. The tribes that used canoes, desired a boatable stream or lake, but a good many prominent sites of the state are situated upon rivulets or near springs and are miles from any point that could be reached by canoe. It is impossible, at this time, to find "live" water near some of the old sites. The interesting inclosures or

[32] Alexander Henry, *Travels and Adventures in Canada and the Indian Territory, 1760-1776* (New York, 1809), pp. 69, 70.

"forts" of Ogemaw County are very near the Rifle River which gave easy communication by canoe with Saginaw Bay. The inclosures, quite similar to those of Ogemaw in Missaukee County, are not near streams and probably a part of the year depended upon impounded water for drinking.

Close proximity to a supply of suitable material for lodges, fires, and other purposes for which wood was required was essential. The lodge-builder had to take precautions against a situation that was liable to be hit by falling trees and limbs. Constant access to the gathering grounds from which foods were collected was all important. The distance which game, fish, and forage had to be transported, especially if canoes were not used, had a limit not exceeding a few miles. A growth of reeds, rushes, flags, long grass, and other swamp-growing plants within the gathering range of a group of wigwams was convenient as a source of material for fabrics of coarse mats, rugs, windbreaks, and covers. The lee side of a ridge or hill was more comfortable in winter than a wind swept open space. Woods, of course, were good windbreaks.

CHIPPEWA COUNTY

The early missionaries and explorers refer to the regions contiguous to the Saint Mary's as being, at times, the rendezvous of many Indians, some say thousands, attracted by the immense numbers of whitefish that appear to have gorged the stream in certain parts. The situation deserves mention as an illustration of the superabundance, in its season, of one particular kind of food upon which the people depended for considerable periods.

SAGINAW VALLEY

Saginaw Valley was the most populous part of the state. There have been identified 120 old villages, in addition to other sites in Saginaw County. Almost 30 per cent of all the Indians of Michigan frequented the counties of Bay, Saginaw, Genesee, Shiawassee, and Tuscola. There was also a good percentage in the valley of the Maple River in Clinton County, which district was contiguous to the Shiawassee. The explanation is easy and pertinent to the discussion. The streams that united to form the Saginaw River and the Saginaw itself, and the lands adjacent were an ideal environment for all that forest Indians might desire. The woods bordering the Shiawassee River between Owosso and Saginaw are thus described by C. C. Douglas, one of the party who went with Douglass Houghton, the first State Geologist, upon a survey through the central parts of the state, in 1837:

> Oaks . . . massive and tall, and centuries old; the elms, the most graceful and majestic of trees of any land; the tulip or whitewood, magnificent in size and height above even the Titans of the forest; the broad and green-leaved linden; the clean-bodied beech; the saccharine maples, so superb in their autumnal dresses, . . .; the giant sycamore, ghost-like, with its white, naked limbs; —these are the common habitants of the forest." [33]

Before the lands were settled by whites, there could be traced many an Indian cornfield, the products of which added materially to the maintenance of the people. The more attention the tribes gave to agriculture the more likely they were to remain in the same part of the country. It will be noted by the chart that the original forest cover of the Saginaw district was predominantly or exclusively hardwood.

NEWAYGO COUNTY

Newaygo County, according to the surveys, had a very numerous Indian population. It was traversed by a wide belt of heavy pine and also contained three or four prairies. Some of the most interesting mound structures of the state

---

[33] *Geological Reports of Douglass Houghton, First State Geologist of Michigan, 1837-1845*, Ed. by George N. Fuller, (The Michigan Historical Commission, Lansing, 1928), pp. 26-27.

were in the vicinity of the Muskegon River which afforded a liberal amount of subsistence. There have also been disclosed in the northeastern part of Oceana and the southwestern part of Lake counties, in the region of the numerous small lakes and the south branch of the Pere Marquette River, evidences of an unusually numerous population. These waters with their rice, fish, fowl, and shore-frequenting animals made the pine woods through which they flowed, and in which they were situated, comfortable for the people although the evergreen forest usually was, as elaborated elsewhere, a kind of no-man's land.

ROSCOMMON COUNTY

Roscommon County is almost in the center of the pine country. It contains Houghton, the largest lake in the state which, together with Higgin's Lake, makes an expanse of water covering 33 square miles. Houghton Lake is very shallow and unusually well adapted to wild rice growth. Although in the midst of the pines, Roscommon County was a comfortable abode for the natives since it possessed large crops of rice, abundance of fish, game, and fowl, and connected by the Muskegon River with a more or less populous country to the southwest. No less than 20 burial mounds, 2 ancient village sites, and an extensive burying ground have been located upon or very near the lake shores.

BERRIEN COUNTY

In number of sites Berrien County is third in the state. Very nearly the same conditions prevailed as in the Saginaw region. The wild rice plant was very abundant in the St. Joseph, and in other streams and alluvial lakes. It was a wonderful fish and game country, and the soil was well adapted to Indian corn culture. These statements apply largely to the western half of the two southern tiers of counties of the state.

FROM THE SAGINAW AND SHIAWASSEE TO THE
SCIOTO AND GREAT MIAMI

If the distribution of sites upon *The Archaeological Atlas of Michigan* and the *Archeological Atlas of Ohio* is checked, it will be observed that they were about uniformly distributed from the streams that unite to form the Saginaw River to the sources of the Scioto and Great Miami rivers in Ohio, a distance of over 250 miles. In the Saginaw country, in central Michigan, for the reason already mentioned, the environment was very congenial to the Indians and they increased in numbers accordingly. In the west-central parts of Ohio, drained by the two rivers mentioned, the conditions for subsistence became more alluring than the expanse of country to the immediate north, and there was a corresponding numerical increase in the primitive population.

ISLE ROYALE

Isle Royale, Keweenaw County, had a number of old village sites. The island was sparsely covered with spruce, balsam, cedar, brush, a few maples, and other deciduous trees peculiar to a rough and rocky surface. It is doubtful, owing to the rigorous climate and the difficulty of obtaining subsistence during the winter, that the Indians who went there remained the year around. It was one of the sources of copper which the natives, with their crude methods of mining, obtained in small quantities. The copper doubtless accounts for the fact of there being so much evidence of occupation. The same is true of other parts of the copper region which must otherwise have been rather forbidding.

THE INDIANS AND THE DUNES

A very interesting study, and one that has not received more than casual attention, could be made of Indian life among the dunes. Almost the entire eastern shore of Lake Michigan is piled with immense ridges of loose drifting sand. The winds sweeping from the lake shift the sand from piles in one place and bank it up in another leaving "blow holes" where, perhaps but a day or two before, there was a sand pile several feet high.

During the milder parts of the year it was the custom of the Indians to assemble in villages in various places, between the dunes and the border of the lake, particularly at the mouths of rivers. Almost all the streams on the west side of Michigan first discharge their waters into small lakes that are separated by only a slight distance from the main lake. The fishing was excellent and in the marshes there were birds and aquatic animals. In the late fall and until early spring the shore villages were generally abandoned for winter quarters upstream and away from the piercing winds and cutting sands as they were driven in whatever direction the breeze might be blowing. The evidences of the foregoing are camping sites, fireplaces, and occasionally skeletons and relics found in the sands. Sometimes human bones, that must have been at times before many feet from the top of the dune, are exposed by the winds. At the mouth of Devil River, in Alpena County, an entire cemetery with large numbers of human skeletons was exposed. The same phenomenon happened at Cross Village and at other places.

FORT BUILDING

In various parts of the state there are ancient inclosures usually referred to as forts, although there is not convincing enough reason to suppose they were built solely as places of defense. Their existence in a territory is not proof that there were great numbers of people to occupy them.

One of the inclosures in Missaukee County is 177 feet in diameter. The banks now average 5 feet in height and are 7 feet across the base. Upon the outside is a moat or ditch from which the earth was taken to construct the embankments. Supposing originally the banks were 10 feet across the base, 5 feet across the top, and 8 feet high, they would have contained very nearly 31,860 cubic feet of earth.

From outward appearance, the earth of which the banks are built was taken from the surrounding trench. The distance for carrying the earth is only the slope from the bottom of the trench to the top of the bank. If one man transported from the trench to the bank one-half cubic foot of dirt at a time, and he did this 40 times a day, it would have required 32 days for 50 men to have built the structure.

There are a number of inclosures, similar to the one just described, in Ogemaw County. The largest is 906 feet in circumference. Supposing the same measurements and working conditions to have prevailed there as for the Missaukee banks, it would have taken 50 men 49 days to make the excavation and pile up the embankment. A few hundred Indians in one summer could have built all the inclosures in the two counties. The supposition that the walls were 10 feet upon the base, 5 feet across the top, and 8 feet high is probably much too liberal an allowance for the actual dimensions. From the appearance of these works at the present time, the conclusion is not warranted that they were more than half the dimensions assumed in the estimate.

Deficiency of the Map

It is impossible to represent upon a single map as many physical features and locations as are desirable for a complete illustration of every point involved. The situations of some of the lakes and streams that had an influencing effect upon habitations have been omitted in order that the timber zones and population districts might stand out more clearly. For example, the southwestern corner of Montmorency County, Albert Township, is within the coniferous belt and has a group of sites explained by the adjacent bodies of water. East and West Twin lakes are situated in this locality. They afforded a sufficient supply of food material to make living near them possible the year around. Reference is made in previous paragraphs to the conditions in the vicinity of Houghton and other lakes in Newaygo and Lake counties.